The Art of the
SCROLL SAW

The Art of the Scroll Saw

Patrick Spielman

Sterling Publishing Co., Inc. New York
A Sterling/Chapelle Book

For Chapelle Limited

Owner: Jo Packham

Staff: Malissa Boatwright, Trice Boerens, Rebecca Christensen, Holly Fuller, Cherie Hanson, Holly Hollingsworth, Susan Jorgensen, Susan Laws, Amanda McPeck, Jamie Pierce, Leslie Ridenour, Cindy Stoeckl, Nancy Whitley, and Lorrie Young.

Photography: Ryne Hazen and Kevin Dilley for Hazen Photography.

Library of Congress Cataloging-in-Publication Data

Spielman, Patrick E.
    The art of the scroll saw / Patrick Spielman
        p.   cm.
    "A Sterling/Chapelle book."
    Includes index.
    ISBN 0-8069-0854-8
    1. Jig saws. 2. Woodwork--Patterns.   I. Title.
  TT 186.S6634 1995   94-47991
  745.51--dc20   CIP

10   9   8   7   6   5   4   3   2   1

Published by Sterling Publishing Company, Inc.
387 Park Avenue South, New York, N.Y. 10016
© 1995 by Chapelle Limited
Distributed in Canada by Sterling Publishing
c/o Canadian Manda Group, One Atlantic Avenue, Suite 105
Toronto, Ontario, Canada M6K 3E7
Distributed in Great Britain and Europe by Cassell PLC
Wellington House, 125 Strand, London WC2R 0BB, England
Distributed in Australia by Capricorn Link (Australia) Pty Ltd.
P.O. Box 6651, Baulkham Hills, Business Centre, NSW 2153, Australia
Printed and Bound in Hong Kong
All right reserved

Sterling ISBN 0-8069-0854-8

Introduction

The scroll saw machine is actually a very elementary woodworking tool originating over a century ago. The modern scroll saw is essentially still an inelaborate and low-tech device. Instead of employing the treadle, or foot-powered drive, of the early saws, present machines convert the rotary action of their electric motor to an up-and-down reciprocal cutting action identical to that of their old predecessors. Scroll saws carry very thin, fine cutting blades. By comparison to other wood machining techniques, scroll saws provide unequalled capabilities for cutting very sharp, delicate curves and squared corners that are seemingly impossible.

When put into the hands of creative people, scroll saws can generate art objects of the highest levels in a wide variety of materials (thin and thick) that can be functional as well as beautiful.

This book is essentially an exhibit of the best works by some of the most widely known and productive scroll saw artists in the U.S. and abroad today. Many of these individuals also offer their techniques and invite the reader to share in the creation of such superb scroll sawn objects for personal use—not for production or profit. The projects vary in skill level and sawing intensity, but most are designed to be made in the home shop with the average scroll saw.

Showcased in the gallery section of the book are some projects that require very involved or specialized techniques originated or perfected by the artist. Some of these more complex and advanced woodworking projects also involve multiple woodworking techniques.

Throughout you will see the boundless capabilities of the scroll saw exhibited. It is the intent of this book to inspire beginners and to allow the advanced or professional to appreciate viewing the exceptional and unprecedented efforts of other artists. Hopefully everyone will sample and experience the distinct delight of creating objects with the scroll saw.

–Patrick Spielman

Contents

Contents

1

An antique scroll saw dating to the 1820's. This, The Star saw, was very similar to others sold under such names as Cricket and New Rogers. Made by the Millers Falls Co., this was probably the most popular of foot-powered treadle saws. It was inexpensive, just $2.50. These saws satisfied the demand for a cheap, foot-

powered saw for the home shop, and presumably it was also sold abroad. It weighed only 17 pounds, was 37" high, had a 17½" throat capacity and a table just 8" in diameter. It featured wooden arms and very efficient quick-release blade clamps with a built-in flip lever tensioning system.

2

The blade clamp and lever tensioning system on the early scroll saws. Designed over 100 years ago, it is still one of the quickest and easiest of all (including those today) to use for clamping and tensioning the blade with no wrenches or set screws. Note how the double pivot linkage of the lever creates blade tension when lifted.

3

The most elegant and sought after by antique collectors is this Barnes Velocipede No. 2 saw. A n industrial quality tool of the late 1800s, it is capable of cutting stock 3" thick at the rate of one foot per minute. Up to one thousand two hundred, 1½" strokes per minute can be achieved. This

saw stands 48" high, has a 24" throat capacity, carries 5" to 7" blades and has a generous 20"-diameter solid wood table. Shown here is an aluminum reproduction model available from the Tool Company of Raymore, Missouri.

4

This modern mid-priced bench-top scroll saw by Delta International features 2 speeds and is capable of cutting from 850 to 1725 cutting strokes per minute. It has a 16" throat and a 2" stock thickness cutting capacity. Other features include a tilting table 11¾" in diameter and newer models have quick blade clamping and tensioning devices.

5

The Excalibur 30 saw has the largest throat capacity available today. This saw features a 30" throat and 2" stock thickness cutting capacity. It offers a constant power variable speed, and cutting action from 60 to 1500 ¾" strokes per minute. One unique feature is the top arm which lifts with an optional foot pedal. This makes it

especially easy to thread the blade down from the top side when making inside cutouts on very large workpieces. This saw also features an effective quick blade clamp and up front lever tensioning device. Excalibur saws are made in Scarborough, Canada ,and distributed in the U.S. by Seyco Sales Co., Garland, Texas.

6

The Hegner saws are credited with the 1970s resurgence of scroll sawing with their introduction of an electrically driven, high-tech engineered machine made of modern metal alloys. Manufactured in Germany, available worldwide and distributed in the U.S. by Advanced Machinery

Imports of New Castle, Delaware, this model 18-V is one of the most popular models among woodworkers. It will cut stock up to 2⅜" thick. It has a 400 to 1700 variable stroke drive and cuts metals and plastics as well as wood. Optional quick-change blade clamps are available.

1

A magnification lamp is a recommended accessory for accurate, precise sawing of fine, detailed work. Shadow-free illumination and line magnification make expert, precise sawing easy.

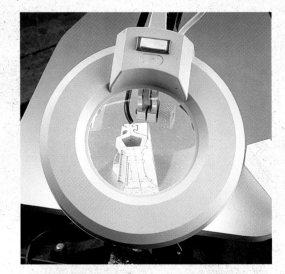

2

The best blade clamps today are of the quick "finger-release" type shown here. Made by Seyco Sales of Garland, Texas, these clamps are available to fit most brands of popular scroll saws, many of which otherwise still require allen wrenches or other cumbersome devices.

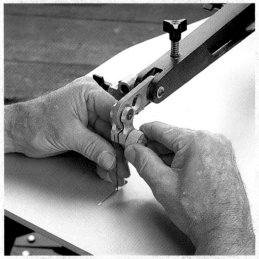

3

Blades: As choices of good sawing machines have recently expanded, so has the choice and performance capabilities of blades. Look for the new skip tooth configurations with reverse lower teeth for smoothest, feather-free cuts. New ground blades with triple skip profiles cut smooth and cool in a variety of wood materials

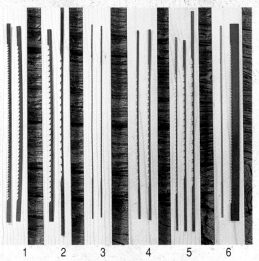

and various thicknesses. Photo compares traditional to new and a range of blade types and sizes.

1. Standard scroll blades
2. Skip tooth blade, Olson thick wood blade skip tooth
3. Olson no. 2 reverse tooth, Eberlie no. 5 skip tooth
4. Hegner no. 9 double tooth skip, Eberlie no. 11 double tooth skip
5. Ground blades - Olson no. 7 PGB blade, Hegner Ultra, Apallo
6. Metal cutting

4

TIP: To increase cutting performance and to extend the life of
larger blades, consider a quick do-
it-yourself sharpening. Make a
simple clamp from 2 pieces of
hinged hardwood. Just a few
quick strokes with a diamond flat
file gives new life to an otherwise
dull blade.

5

TIP: Round and remove the sharp
corners at the back of the blade.
Use a fine abrasive such as this
diamond stone or a very fine file.
This will minimize friction in tight
radius cuts, increase blade life,
and make zero radius turning eas-

ier. Also experiment with a stone
to cautiously touch up the side of
cheaper (non-ground) blades to
remove burrs caused from metal
flow of the stamping process during manufacturing.

6

Some recommended safety
accessories include ear, eye and
respiratory protection devices. A
foot switch is not only useful to
speed up fretwork and repetitive
interior cutting, but it permits the
operator to maintain consistent
control of the workpiece with both
hands.

7

TIP: Use a proportion wheel when enlarging or reducing patterns on a copy machine. This is simply two circular, rotating scales. Align the mark of the existing size on the inner wheel to the mark of the new desired size on the outer disk. The percentage to set the copy machine is given in the square window of the proportion wheel.

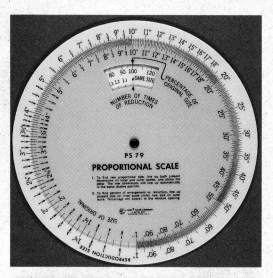

8

TIP: This flutter wheel consisting of special abrasive sheets mounted on an arbor is ideal for removing feathering and softening sharp edges. It is available from Klingspor's Sanding Catalog, Hickory, North Carolina.

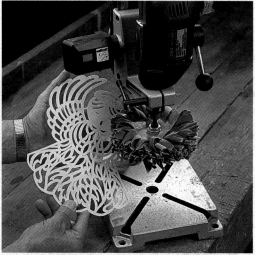

9

TIP: Checking the relationship between various degrees of saw table tilt for inlay, marquetry and dimensional relief work. Simply make small oval cuts inward from the edge as shown and slip the waste piece up or down until it is

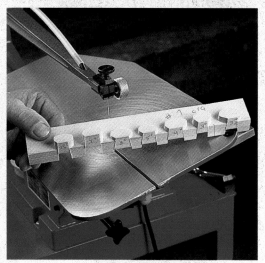

wedged against the kerf. Use scrap stock of the same thickness as the project. Mark each cut indicating the table tilt adjustment used in degrees and also mark the brand and size blade used to make the cuts.

Artists

Patrick and Patricia Spielman

Patrick and Patricia Spielman (known among friends as Mr. and Mrs. Pat) live surrounded by natural forest in the famous tourist area of Door County in northeast Wisconsin. Mr. Pat, a 1958 graduate of the University of Wisconsin–Stout, taught high school and vocational woodworking in Wisconsin public schools for 27 years.

Today, the Pats own *Spielman's Wood Works* and *Spielman's Kid Works*. Both are gift galleries that offer high-quality hand- and machine-crafted wood products produced locally and from around the world.

The Spielman woodworking activities are by and large a cooperative family effort. Patricia is not only the business manager and buyer for the galleries, but she is also an artist who creates many original scroll saw and wood project designs that appear in this volume and many of the other Spielman books. Their son, Robert, and his wife, Anne, have their own wood product business, creating wood signs, furniture, and personalized wooden mailboxes. Their daughters, Sherri and Sandra, are both graphic artists and often help their dad prepare art and manuscripts for publishers.

Patrick's love for wood and woodworking began between the ages of 8 and 10, when he transformed wooden fruit crates into toys. Encouragement from his parents, two older brothers, and a sister, who provided basic tools to keep the youngster occupied, enabled Patrick to become a very productive woodworker at an early age. "I owned a Montgomery Ward scroll saw before I was 11 years old," he says.

Patrick left the school classroom 10 years ago, but he continues to teach and share ideas and designs through his published works. He has written over 50 woodworking books with some translated into Dutch and German. About half of the titles are dedicated to the subject of the scroll saw, "a safe, interesting, and fun to use machine" says Patrick, adding that its potential is still to be fully exploited.

One of Patrick's proudest accomplishments is his book, *The Router Handbook,* which has sold over 1½ million copies worldwide. His updated version, *The New Router Handbook,* was selected the best how-to book of 1994 by the National Association of Home and Workshop writers.

Woodworking has been very good to the Pat Spielmans, and they receive great satisfaction in giving back by helping others find and experience the pure joy and pleasure of working with wood. One of the quickest and easiest ways to accomplish that is with a very simple, but extremely remarkable device–the scroll saw.

Bertha Bluhm's father came to America in 1922, bringing with him his fretwork patterns and tools. As she grew up, Bertha watched her father make many beautiful pieces. When her father passed away, she felt that someone should learn the uncommon craft . Although she now uses mostly electric machines, Bertha began learning fretwork with hand tools and some of her father's original patterns.

Bertha specializes in miniatures, as you can see in her featured doll furniture. "Fretwork was very popular during the Victorian Age and I try to create pieces in color and design that could have been found in someone's home during that time," she says.

Bertha has been featured as local "Artist of the Month" and enjoys giving demonstrations using her hand tools. "I am very pleased to see the renewed interest in this art form and the availability of more tools and patterns," she says.

Working in their southwest Wisconsin studio, dubbed The Art Factory, Dirk and Karen Boelman treat scroll sawers around the globe to an ever increasing array of challenging patterns. In just over 6 years, Dirk has produced over 3,000 patterns. His work appears in over a dozen books by Patrick Spielman, and many other woodworking magazines and catalogs. Dirk has also made a major contribution to preserving and resurrecting century-old patterns, preventing them from being lost to history.

Dirk's wife, Karen, is also an accomplished designer and developer of fabulous scroll sawn projects. She spends much of her time producing completed projects for retail sales as well as working at their mail-order business.

For the past nine years at Boyers' Woods, located in Oregon, Illinois, Bob and Marie have created many treasured pieces of work. The scroll saw has become their foundation, inspiring their hammers, bats and custom work. Both self-taught woodworkers, they combine their creativity: Bob with his unique lettering style and Marie with her unusual designs. Together, they produce pieces that are truly special.

Hammers and bats are an immense challenge in that the thickness, shape and hardness of the wood often makes them difficult to scroll-saw. Through many years of experience, Bob has conquered what once was a difficult task.

The Boyers' work has expanded to worldwide with some of their pieces exhibited in Russia and Germany. Their work has also been seen in *Country Magazine* and at Holzfest, one of the Midwest's greatest wood shows in Amana, Iowa.

In the mid-sixties at the age of 10, Rolf Brunner was introduced to fretwork in his hometown of Zurich, Switzerland. As part of a family Christmas project, he cut simple patterns with a hand-held saw. His mother carefully painted and finished them to be given as gifts.

Rolf continued to dabble in all types of woodwork, but his interest in fretwork was rekindled while working as an industrial arts teacher. He was asked to cut out a pattern on the scroll saw and, from that point on, he began searching to find quality patterns and fellow fretworkers.

Rolf has been working full-time as a fretworker for three years. Some of his work has earned him numerous awards, such as "best in show" and several first places. He has begun to design his own patterns, many of which can be found in his first book, *The Fretwork Shop*.

A native of Wisconsin, Kevin Clarkowski has been doing woodwork since 1983. After earning a Bachelor's degree from the University of Massachusetts-Lowell in accounting, Kevin worked in the credit union industry. On his 40th birthday, he quit his job to work full-time at his woodworking.

In 1989, Kevin formed his own company, *Pro Wood*, which does a variety of custom work and prototypes. The company has done set work on *The Dillenger* movie and is the main supplier of custom bases for George Watts & Sons crystal. One of his definitive bases is on display at the Experimental Aviation and Aircraft museum in Wisconsin.

Kevin's scroll saw work demonstrates a unique view and expertise in the art of negative cut design and templates.

Gösta Dahlqvist was born in 1918 in a small town in Sweden. His father was a craftsman who made clogs and Gösta worked in the same factory as a young boy. In the 1930s, Gösta started experimenting with figure sawing and it became a lifelong hobby. He used a common, simple bow saw, cutting patterns shown in a weekly magazine, the *Aller's Family Journal*.

Gösta worked in the engineering industry for almost 40 years and it wasn't until his retirement at age 60 that he really concentrated on his sawing. At that time he found a Hegner saw and today owns three of them in different sizes.

His interest in figure sawing increased when he sent away for several books by Patrick Spielman. "My own creativity increases when I see and read about other's ideas. I have made a lot of friends through my sawing," he says. Gösta has been engaged by Hegner saws in Sweden to show his work at numerous exhibitions.

Nancy Holewinski started woodworking as a child with her first projects being balsa wood airplanes. Her continued interest in wood led her to fretwork, which she excels in today.

Fretwork patterns are very intricate and Nancy enjoys the challenge of the many small cuts. Her husband, Don, assembles all of her pieces while Nancy adds her personal touches, such as velvet lining in her boxes.

Nancy has been involved in many craft shows. She considers fretwork an art form that she *loves*.

Julie Kiehnau was born and raised in Door County, Wisconsin. Her father sold firewood and owned a lot of wooded land. As a child, Julie would work with her father in the woods and shared his love for the unique smells and features of wood.

Julie enrolled in a woodworking class while attending Gibraltar High School. Her instructor was Patrick Spielman. "My woodworking then pertained only to basic band-saw cutting, some lathe work and a lot of sanding," she admits. In 1985, Julie began working at Spielman's Woodworks Gift Shop. There, she was introduced to the scroll saw. Silhouettes are Julie's favorite projects to work on. She has a feeling of satisfaction when the solid wood is transformed into a finished piece.

Besides scroll sawing, Julie enjoys working on the family farm operated by her husband, being outdoors and spending time with her two children.

For the past 15 years, Dan Kihl has been making a living with a scroll saw. Starting out in Wisconsin, where Dan had his own gift shop, a friend gave him an old scroll saw. Since he was in need of products to sell, Dan combined his natural artistic ability with his own love of nature and began creating his own innovative designs.

In 1988, Dan, his wife, and their two children moved to Arizona. He became immediately inspired by the area's natural beauty, wildlife, and Native-American heritage. There, he developed several unique sculptural processes utilizing the scroll saw and other materials that capture the spirit of the Southwest. From Dan's vast library of designs, he has developed several highly successful pieces that are now being wholesaled to the gift industry all over the country.

Roy King and Scott Kochendorfer have been friends since the first grade and share a common bond. They are both self-taught scroll sawers and they LOVE the art. Together they started Scroller LTD and have been developing their unique 3-D scroll saw patterns for about 2 years. Their projects are easy and fun to do and each of their over 500 patterns is complete with details to make the projects "come alive."

They have been featured in *Better Homes and Gardens Wood Magazine* and they have appeared on *The American Workshop*.

"Our goal is to elevate scroll sawing to new heights as never seen before by developing imaginative, fun and challenging patterns. We like to call it–painting with a scroll saw," says Roy.

Silas Kopf was born in 1949 in Warren, Pennsylvania. After studying architecture at Princeton University, he apprenticed for Wendell Castle. In 1988, he received the National Endowment for the Arts Craftsmanship Fellowship and studied with Pierre Ramond at the Ecole Boulle in Paris.

His designs have been exhibited

in galleries and museums across the country and are held in private collections nationwide.

Kopf has been an instructor and lecturer on marquetry at craft schools and universities around the United States. He is the founder and director of the Woodworkers Alliance for Rainforest Protection (WARP).

As a young boy, Rick Longabaugh can remember being intrigued by one of his father's hobbies–restoring the wood framing on antique cars. As Rick grew, woodworking continued to be an enjoyable and rewarding part of his life–from shop classes in high school to the woodworking pattern business he and his wife, Karen, run called The Berry Basket. In the past 2 years, they have self-published 4 pattern books. They also offer a wide variety of unique patterns and accessories through their mail-order catalog. Rick was featured on the cover of *Popular Woodworking* in November of 1993, and in March of 1994 the same magazine published an article on the business side of The Berry Basket.

"As I design," explains Rick, "I strive to create a balance between the aesthetics of the pattern and the beauty of the wood. Of all the design themes I use (Southwest, Country, Wildlife, etc.), my personal favorite is florid Victorian ornament with its graceful lines that recapture an era of days gone by."

Steve Malavolta is a self-taught woodworker who specializes in designing and creating hardwood jigsaw puzzles. Using his inlaying techniques with select hardwoods, semi-precious stones and metals, he creates abstracts, landscape scenes and architectural sculptural puzzles.

To Steve, a good puzzle must first be visually appealing and then challenging. Layering puzzles is something that is unique to Steve's style, not only creating depth to the design, but increasing the difficulty. Finishing is also important to Steve because it creates puzzle pieces enjoyable to hold and manipulate into place.

"I have always incorporated function into my artwork and each puzzle is made with the intent to be played, creating both entertainment and intellectual challenge," says Steve. "My goal as a woodworker is to present my puzzles as enjoyable art of heirloom quality."

Jeffrey Alan Nelson was born in Grand Rapids, Michigan. He is the proud father of three and presently resides in Ossining, New York. He has been designing and creating fine marquetry for the past 14 years. Jeff incorporates his designs into custom furnishings as well as architectural installations. A 6' x 11' piece of Jeff's marquetry was recently finished for a distinguished Spanish artist now residing in Puerto Rico.

Jeff majored in design, sculpture and painting at Macomb College in Warren, Michigan, and the San Francisco Art Institute in California. He has participated in shows and exhibitions all over the country, where his awards have ranged from Best of Show, Best of Wood, and 1st, 2nd, and 3rd places.

John and Sheila Polhemus produce and market a line of scroll sawn pieces under the name of JP Woodworks. Their work has been featured in several books by Patrick Spielman, and such magazines as *Woodshop News* and *Creative Woodwork and Crafts*. They have received an award of recognition in the field of Fine Arts and Crafts from the governor of their home state, Maryland, as well as many awards at various fairs and shows.

John's addiction to dimensional puzzles led to the acquisition of his first scroll saw to reproduce old wooden puzzles for his collection. He began selling his puzzles at local craft shows to make money to pay for materials and more puzzles. This exposure led to the current line they exhibit today. Sheila excels in the design process, using requests received from the public as her inspiration.

Carla Radsek's woodworking projects range from small pieces of jewelry and jewelry boxes to gingerbread fretwork for houses. All are crafted in a small workshop in her rural Mondovi, Wisconsin home.

Carla is a self-taught woodworker who picked up the hobby from books while staying at home with her two small children. Her skills have developed into a small business called Fretwork Fancy, with assistance in sanding and staining from her husband, Steve. Detailed patterns and designs are Carla's speciality. "The more ornate and delicate the design," she says, "the better I like it." Carla has been featured in articles in many local newspapers and magazines. "This kind of work appeals to me," she reflects, "and I find it relaxing. There's something new to make all the time and it's a nice feeling to know that I'm leaving something behind for future generations to enjoy–creating family heirlooms."

Kirk Ratajesak, also known as "The Fretworker," has been doing scroll sawing since 1973. After years of doing scrollwork as a craft, Kirk's main emphasis has been in the miniatures field. Most of his designs are his own. Kirk's workmanship and knowledge has been published in many magazines and publications. Kirk wrote a feature article for *The Scale Cabinetmaker* in 1982 that explained fretwork and how it is done. His work has been at top miniature shows throughout the country as well as art galleries and miniature museums.

In January of 1992, Kirk completed a 1' x 16' mural for the main entrance at the Beloit Corporation Headquarters in Beloit, Wisconsin. Other pieces of his artistry can be found in all 50 states and more than 12 countries.

James Reidle has been doing fancy woodwork along with other fine craft work all his life. He grew up watching his father create magnificent pieces of scroll saw fretwork and other unique projects. Reidle has co-authored five scroll saw books with Patrick Spielman. He is especially proud of their book, Scroll Saw Fretwork Techniques & Projects, *which he says is "the bible of fretwork."*

In 1985, Reidle developed the first mail-order scroll-saw-business in several years, known as Wildwood Designs, *that is mainly devoted to fretwork patterns and supplies. His wife, Elaine, and son, Bill, are involved in the business. Plans are in progress for a new museum for the collection of fine scroll work and other items. "My goal in life is to help bring out the talent and creativity of those who love woodworking," says Reidle.*

Judy Gale Roberts, born in Houston, Texas, is a noted artist whose work has received national and international awards. She studied art as a child with her parents. She opted for practical "hands on" apprenticeship with master artist Pat Dudley Roberts. She alsostudied at the Museum of Fine Arts school in Houston.

In the past decade, she has led the revival of an antique art form called intarsia. Judy is currently teaching intarsia to a worldwide audience. She has published the first intarsia instructional book and video and was featured in Better Homes and Gardens Wood Magazine.

"Intarsia fulfills a creative need in me," says Judy. "I enjoy sculpture and working with a variety of wood colors, and I have found a technique that is a union of the two." Judy's works are held in private and corporate collections throughout North America and Europe.

Rob and Kim Russell's shared love of wood led them to start their own woodworking business over 15 years ago. They still enjoy working together—combining Rob's technical skill with Kim's flair for design. "We take great pride in our unique designs, quality work and personal service," says Kim.

Kim and Rob also share a deep love of nature. As often as they can, they escape with their daughter, Neara, for fun in the outdoors. This love is often reflected in their work. Animals, flowers and snowflakes are frequent models for their ornaments, sculpture and utilitarian household objects.

The Russell's work appears in shops and galleries across the country. Lately they have been designing for publishers. "We've been specializing in scroll saw designs since there is so much demand for our style of work —objects that are intricate and attractive yet functional," says Rob.

Jim Shirley knows wood. As a young boy on his parent's farm, he worked it as a hobby. Later, he became a building contractor. Now retired, Jim says, "I was always more interested in old wood than new. Seeing old architecture destroyed just made me heartsick and I wanted to find a way to preserve the old scenes and the grand old buildings." Jim started salvaging and collecting old wood. Wanting to make his collection memorable, he created a rustic landscape from some of his favorite pieces. Interest in his work has grown to the point that his three sons—Lex, Gil, and Todd—work full-time to keep up with demand. Growing up beside their father's wood art, they have each become very skilled, inventive and artistic, putting individ-

ual expression into each piece. From their shop in Rexburg, Idaho, the Shirleys create the masterpieces from Mother Nature's natural palette of woods. They do nothing to enhance or color the wood that they use.

The Shirleys have been featured in *Better Homes and Gardens Wood Magazine*, Utah's television show *Prime Time Access*, as well as other television and newspaper articles. They do about 40 shows a year around the country.

In 1978, Hal and Chloe Smith left the business world, where Hal was a psychotherapist and Chloe a legal secretary, to form their visual arts company, Puma and The White Buffalo. Their unique designs are drawn directly onto the wood by Chloe and then cut by Hal and his son, Sterling, on Excalibur scroll saws.

Their work has taken them to Germany, where they studied further in the art of pierce carving. Their works are hanging at the U.S. Embassy in Paris, the Senate in Athens, and at the foot of Mt. Vesuvius.

Seen at craft shows from New York to California, their work has been warmly accepted by crowds and by producers of some of the finest shows in the country.

For more than 20 years, Gus Stefureac has devoted his time and expertise to his great love and hobby—woodworking. During that time, he has been a member of the prestigious 100 craftsmen in The Village of Yesteryear, NC State Fair, winning a coveted award from his peers for his toys and his presentation.

After 35 years with IBM, Gus retired to work full-time creating toys for children and teaching the use of the scroll saw. He has been featured in woodworking television shows, magazines and many workshops.

The love of history has certainly influenced the toys Gus creates. Selecting designs from his extensive collection of antiques, he provides toys to expand the imagination, develop hand-eye coordination, and, most important, entertain.

Carl Weckhorst started doing fretwork about 35 years ago. His first piece was a wall clock he saw pictured in *Workbench Magazine*. He wrote to the man whose clock was featured and asked him if he would sell him his pattern. Twelve patterns later, Carl was on his way. Until he retired in 1986, Carl did his fretwork part-time. He never went fishing because his love of sawing kept him too busy.

Carl's 5 room house is full of fretwork. His collection includes 40 clocks, three of which are grandfather clocks. One of his clocks stands 7 feet tall and has over 4,000 cutouts. Carl believes he has done over 100,000 cutouts in fretwork. "My dream is to someday see all my fretwork in a museum," he says.

Gerald (Jerry) Wheeler was born and raised in Montana. He began his woodworking at 5 years of age when his father gave him his first tools. During World War II, he made toy airplanes and guns from apple crates for himself and his playmates. He later gained a Bachelor of Science degree in Industrial Arts from Montana State University and a Master of Arts from George Washington University. He taught Industrial Arts and Crafts at the high school level, supplementing his income by selling his work. Upon his retirement in 1983, Jerry became a full-time crafter.

Jerry usually follows a Western or Native American motif in his work. He uses native woods which have been downed—never cutting live trees. He encapsulates the wood in dyed epoxy resin, found metals and turquoise.

Wheeler's work has been featured in several articles, most recently in the September 1993 issue of *World of Wood*.

Robin Wirtz had never seen a scroll saw until her husband brought one home in 1991. Six months later, she didn't know how she had gone so long without one. Robin started using patterns from books and magazines and then went on to designing her own patterns.

Ash is Robin's wood of choice because of its flexibility to hold up to some of her smaller cuts and its light color which is preferable when air brushing. Robin's husband helps with the creative process by preparing the wood from start to finish.

People tell Robin that her love for scroll sawing is evident in her work. "All I know is that it has become a very important part of my life and I hope to be able to continue to produce pieces that people enjoy," she says.

Marc T. Young's marquetry work is found in homes and collections from coast to coast and in several foreign countries. Most of Marc's work is done in hardwood floors, which makes him a rare breed, since there is less than a handful of people who cut marquetry by hand in floors in the entire world.

Studying the works of his mentor, Pierre Ramond of Paris, France, Marc has accomplished all forms of marquetry: Boule marquetry, stone marquetry, traditional marquetry (wood in wood), and even scagliola marquetry, which is very rare. "One of my greatest finds came from studying the work of the late Russian marqueter, Vassilieffe." says Marc. "From his work, I learned to inlay without any gaps or seams."

After four decades of life, Marc feels there is much more to learn and do. He will soon be opening a school for the art of marquetry.

Projects

Chess Set
Patrick and Patricia Spielman

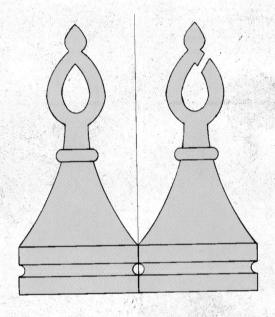

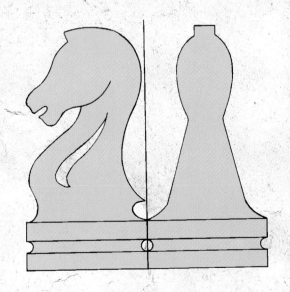

Patterns full size.

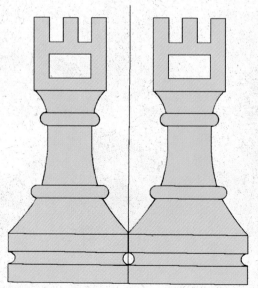

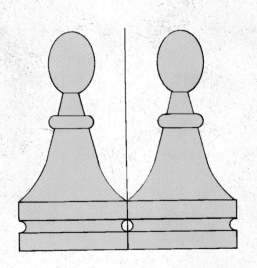

Patterns full size.

1

The chess-piece blocks are first squared to finished length. A ⅛" round-nose bit is used in the router table to make the identical decorative cove cuts around the bottom of all pieces as shown. Note the use of the pusher block.

2

Next, apply the patterns to the adjoining surfaces of the work-piece. Tip: Sharply crease the pattern before applying the temporary bonding adhesive spray.

3

Drill blade entry holes as required. First cut out all inside openings, working from two surfaces, and discard the waste pieces. Next, make two continuous cuts on each face, beginning each from the top of

the chess piece and sawing toward the bottom. Here, the second cut on the first face is almost completed. At the completion of this cut, you will have 3 separate pieces: the part and two waste pieces cut off of each side.

4

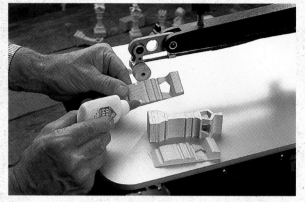

Very carefully place just 4 drops of glue strategically located on the waste pieces so that they will not come in contact with the chess piece when hand-pressed together. Reposition the waste pieces and allow the glue to set 5 to 10 minutes. Clamps are not necessary, but rubber bands may be helpful.

5

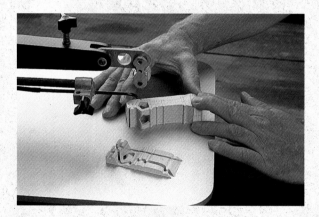

To make the second set of two continuous vertical cuts, rotate the workpiece 90 degrees on the worktable so that the second surface with the pattern is up. Shown here is one cut completed with the waste cut free and the second cut on the second face just underway.

COUNTRY STYLE
FLOWERS
FIONNA HILL

Woodland Hanger Set
Patrick and Patricia Spielman

Suggested material: ¾" thick aromatic cedar.
A metal screw hook can be purchased from
Meisel Hardware Specialties, Mound, Minnesota.

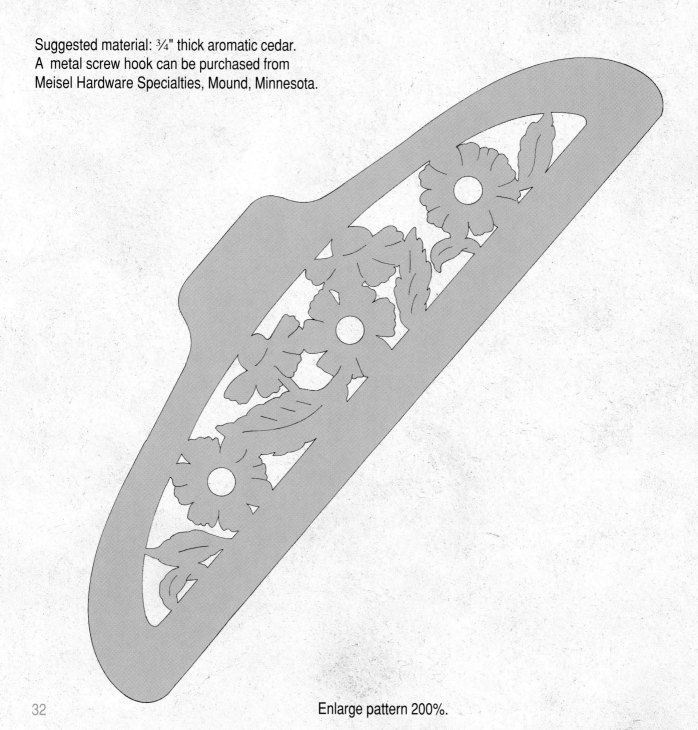

Enlarge pattern 200%.

Clucking Rooster
Patrick and Patricia Spielman

Cut all pieces from
¾"-thick wood.
Round over all edges
at ³⁄₁₆" radius, using
hand tools or a small
router. Finish pieces
individually before
assembling. You can
use pattern and pho-
tos as a guide for
color. Glue all pieces
to a thin backing mate-
rial that is cut slightly
smaller than overall
profile.

Enlarge pattern 200%.

Clucking Rooster
Patrick and Patricia Spielman

Pattern Reduced 50%.

Standing Elegant Angel
Patrick and Patricia Spielman

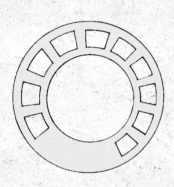

Enlarge Angel pattern 200%. Halo is full size.

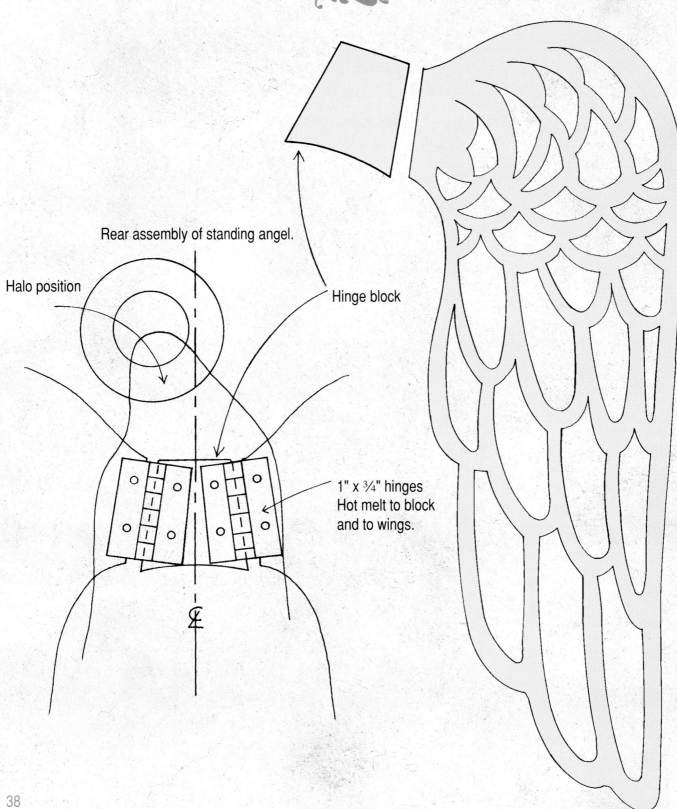

Rear assembly of standing angel.

Halo position

Hinge block

1" x ¾" hinges
Hot melt to block
and to wings.

CL

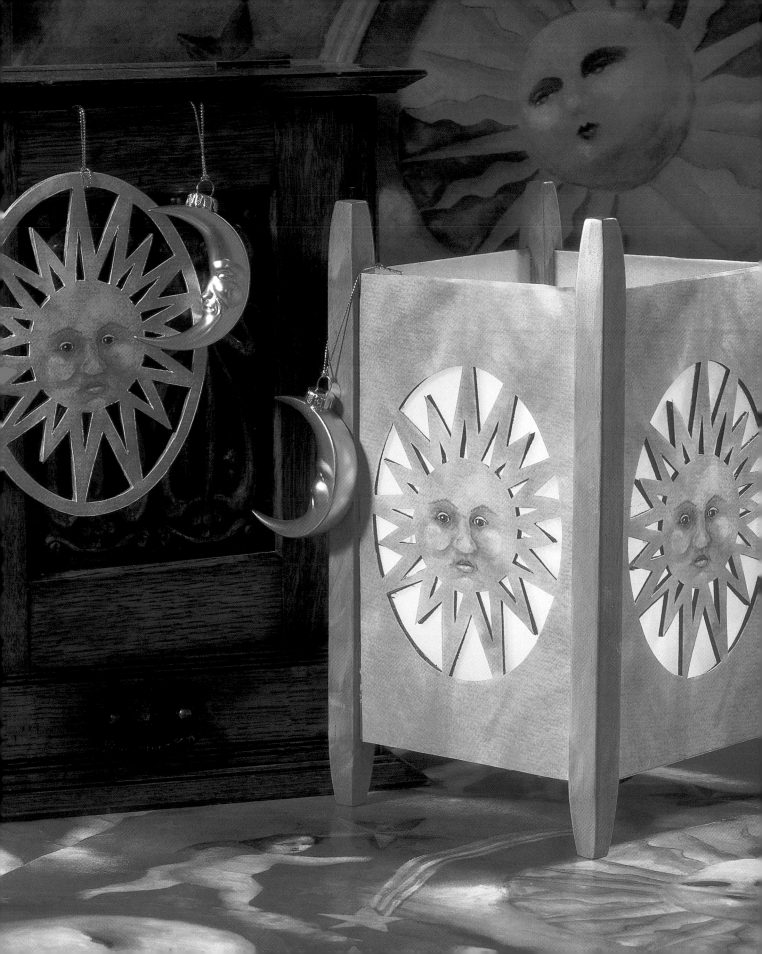

Sunburst Lamp
Patrick and Patricia Spielman

Pattern full size.

A piece of ⅛" plywood holds the lamp socket. This piece fits into a small kerf cut across the inside corners of each leg on the table saw. Use a V-block to hold the work. Guide each leg through the saw with the bot-

tom of the leg against the table saw fence with the supporting V-block held against the miter gauge. Note the completed leg with the stopped grooves and the bottom cut for the ⅛" plywood shown in the background.

Decoupage Instructions:

Make four color photo-copies of the art on page 42. Cut out art to fit sides of lamp and match cut outs.

Combine one-part water an one-part white craft glue. Mix well. Dip small paint-brush into glue-water mixture and thoroughly cover the back of one cutout piece of art.

Lay onto side of lamp. Press completely down with fingertips to squeeze out air bubbles. Smooth the excess glue with fingertips. Let dry completely.

Continue decoupaging art onto other sides of lamp, allowing each side to dry completely.

Sun, Moon, and Stars Utility Box
Patrick and Patricia Spielman

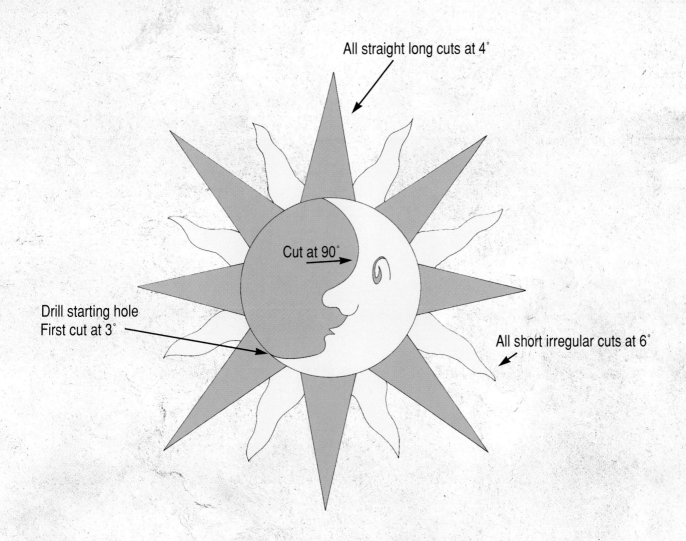

All straight long cuts at 4°

Cut at 90°

Drill starting hole
First cut at 3°

All short irregular cuts at 6°

Enlarge pattern 200%.

1

Make all the longer, straight cuts with the table tilted to 4 degrees. It may be helpful to number the back of each piece for easier orientation during subsequent reassembly.

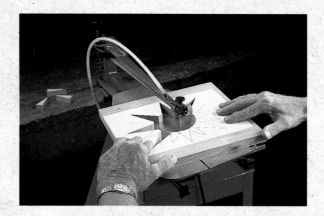

2

One method of rounding over all the pieces is to use a small flush trim router with a special clear plastic, self-made base that provides zero or minimal clearance around this 3/16" radius high-speed roundover bit.

3

Maintain downward pressure during routing. Note that the workpiece is held secure on a thin non-slip router pad. Sand all pieces smooth. Glue pieces into original location raised in relief. Finish box as desired.

Doll Furniture
Bertha Bluhm

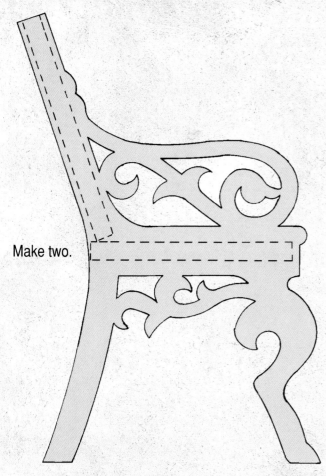

Make two.

Seat can be covered with colored fabric.

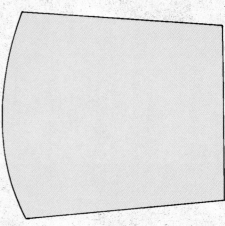

Bevel outermost edges (slightly) to match angle of side pieces produced by seat.

All furniture patterns full size.

Use ³⁄₁₆"-thick material. Seat can be covered with colored fabric.

Bevel outermost edges of back piece (slightly) to fit.

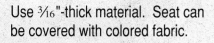

Make two.

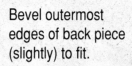

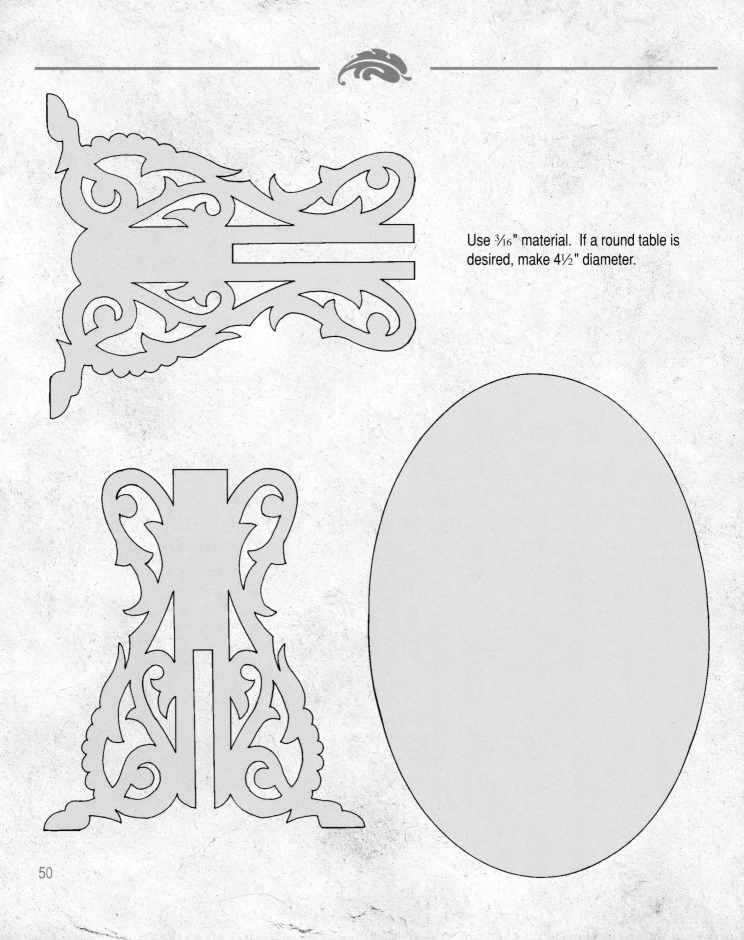

Use ³⁄₁₆" material. If a round table is desired, make 4½" diameter.

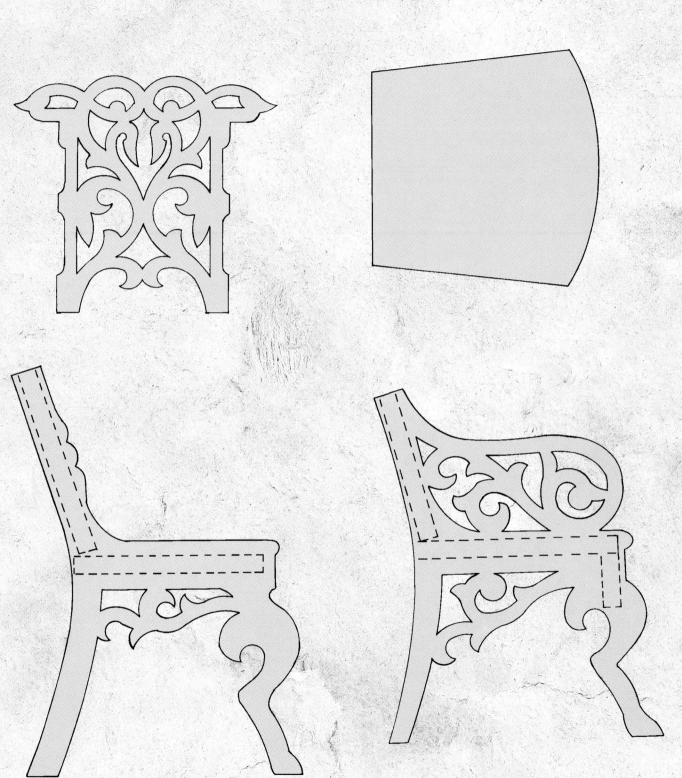

Cinderella Sleigh
Dirk and Karen Boelman

Designed for ¼" thick material.

1. Runners, make two.

2. Cross members, make two.

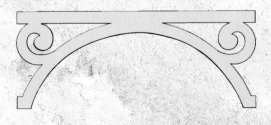

Enlarge patterns 200%.

With good gluing procedures, the project can be assembled entirely with glue; however, you may want to also use additional types of fasteners. Small wire brads, screws or dowels can be used to help strengthen joints.

Give extra attention to the joints where runners (1, page 53) fasten to cross members (2, page 53). Proper assembly of these four pieces is crucial. Runners must be parallel, even at front and back, with the cross members positioned squarely in between and at right angles to the runners.

The sleigh body (parts 3 through 10) mounts on top of the cross members. Dotted lines on the pattern for the bottom panel (4) show proper locations for the cross members (2) beneath the bottom.

Proper positions of all parts that fit between the side panels.

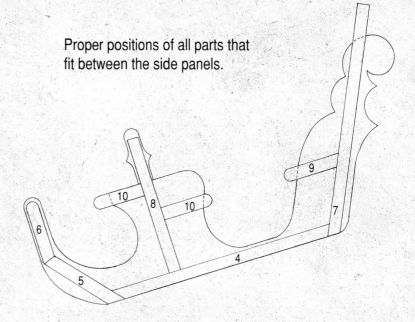

3. Side panels, make two.

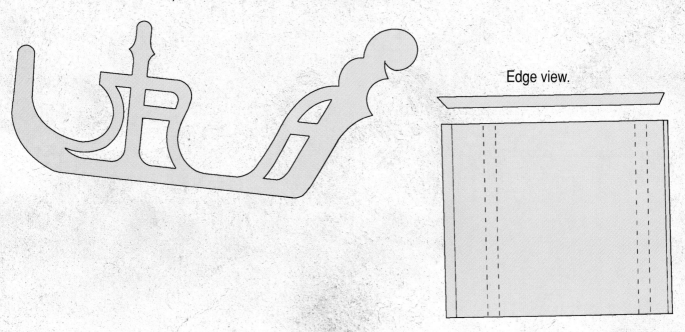

Edge view.

Enlarge patterns 200%.

4. Bottom.

6. Upper front panel.

5. Lower front panel.

Edge view.

Edge view.

8. Divider panel.

7. Back.

Edge view.

Edge view.

9. Rear seat.

Edge view.

10. Front and middle seats, make two.

Edge view.

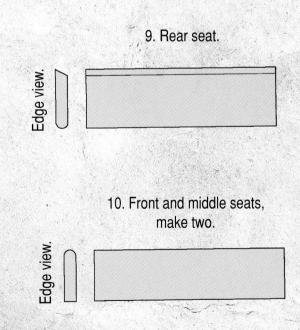

Enlarge patterns 200%.

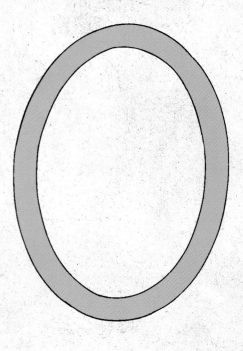

Enlarge candle 200%.

Enlarge Angel, Star and Cross 200%.
© 1993 Dirk Boelman

Gold Leaf Christmas Ornaments
Dirk and Karen Boelman

These ornaments are designed to be made from ⅛" thick material. Solid wood, plywood, or acrylic are equally good choices. Before cutting, check the actual thickness of the material you will be using. Since thicknesses vary, adjust the width of the halved joints on the pattern. The joints should fit snugly.

After cutting each section of the ornament, test halved-joints for fit. Touch up with a file or sandpaper. Separate and apply a small amount of glue to inside edges of the joint with a toothpick or similar device. Reassemble and let dry. Completed ornaments can be finished as desired.

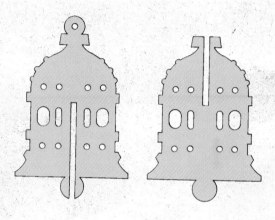

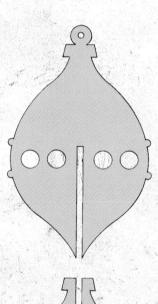

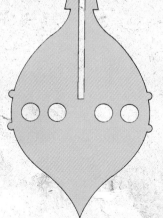

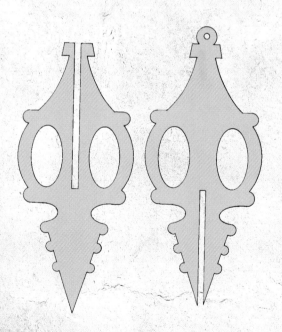

Enlarge patterns 200%.
© Dirk Boelman

Gold Leafing:

Paint your ornament red iron oxide, barn red or venetian red with acrylic paint. The reddish color enhances the gold leaf. Let dry. Spray ornament with spray adhesive. Allow it to set for a minute or two. Apply the gold leaf following manufacture's directions. Brush gently with a dry paintbrush so that the gold leaf adheres to the surface. Remember that as soon as the gold leaf touches the adhesive, it becomes permanent. If you do not get complete coverage, apply more gold leaf. Leaving some of the red color to show through gives an antique look. Allow ornament to dry thoroughly—usually 24 hours.

Enlarge patterns 200%.
© Dirk Boelman

Hammer Handles and Baseball Bat
Bob and Marie Boyer

ABCDEFGHIJKLM
NOPQRSTUVWXYZ

abcdefghijklmnopq
rstuvwxyz

1234567890

Reduce or enlarge letters as needed.

1

Start with a good solid wood-handled hammer. Wrap the head of the hammer with masking tape to prevent marring during the cutting process.

2

Sand the handle to remove the outer finish.

3

Choose a letter design that will fit on your hammer. Draw the letters on paper first for easier placement on the handle. Favoring the thickest part of the handle, use carbon or transfer paper to trace the lettering in place. If you will be using a design, transfer it at this time.

4

A simple jig is required to prevent the hammer from rolling. One can be made from 2 pieces of scrap wood approximately 1⅛" wide by 15" long by ½" thick. These pieces are then hinged and/or bolted and clamped together to ensure that the hammer lies flat. (See photo.)

5

Drill the starting holes inside and around the lettering. These holes should be only slightly larger than the blade being used. Either a #7 or #9 blade works well for cutting hickory handles. The scroll saw speed should be set at 1300 to 1400 strokes per minute, depending on the scroll saw and the operator's comfort.

6

The cutting begins with creating a void above and across the tops of the letters, starting at the outside of the first letter, continuing to the last letter, and returning to the starting point. Next, make the cuts around each letter, leaving just the bottoms of the letters attached. If you used a design, cut this out now.

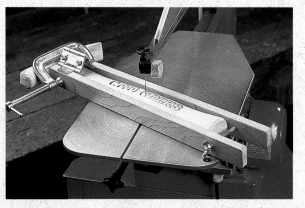

7

Remove the hammer from the jig. With a small file, remove any unwanted marking or protrusions from within the cut area.

8

You may finish by sanding the handle and polishing the head with steel wool, then spraying with a semi-gloss finish, or you may follow our finishing instructions for the hammers in photo.

Feminine Handle
1. Soak handle in green dye.
2. Patina hammer head following manufacturer's instructions on patina medium.
3. With hunter green acrylic paint, paint a ring between handle and head.

Masculine Handle
1. Paint handle brown.
2. Thin down cream-colored paint with water and "whitewash" over the handle.
3. Paint the letters with brick-colored acrylic paint.

Closing Picture Frame
Rolf Brunner

Enlarge pattern 200%.

Name Plate
Kevin Clarkowski

Enlarge pattern 125%.

Cherry Baskets
Gösta Dahlqvist

Use ¼" thick material.

Make two.

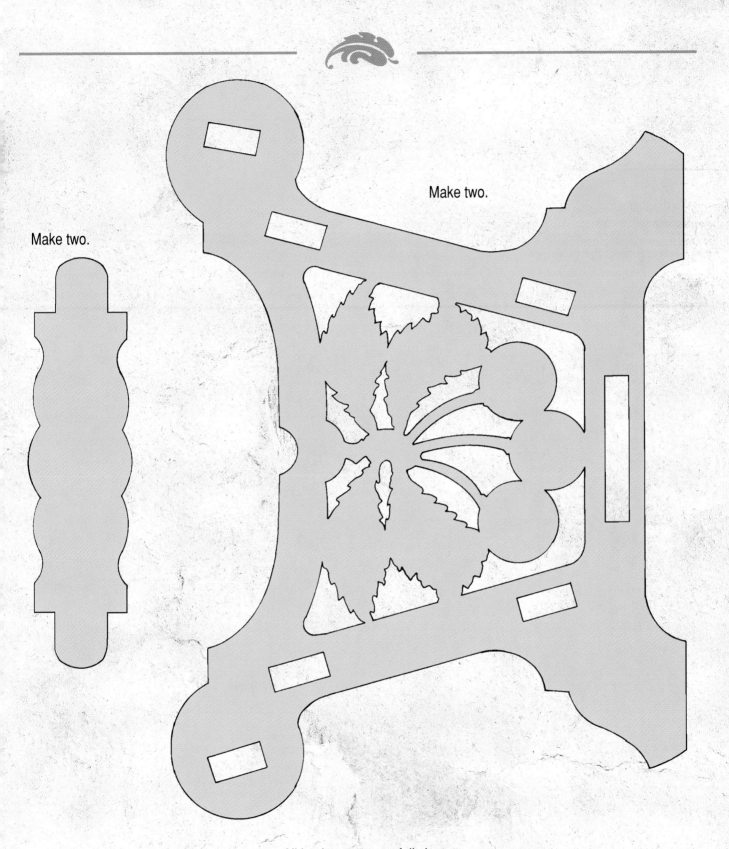

Make two.

Make two.

All basket patterns full size.

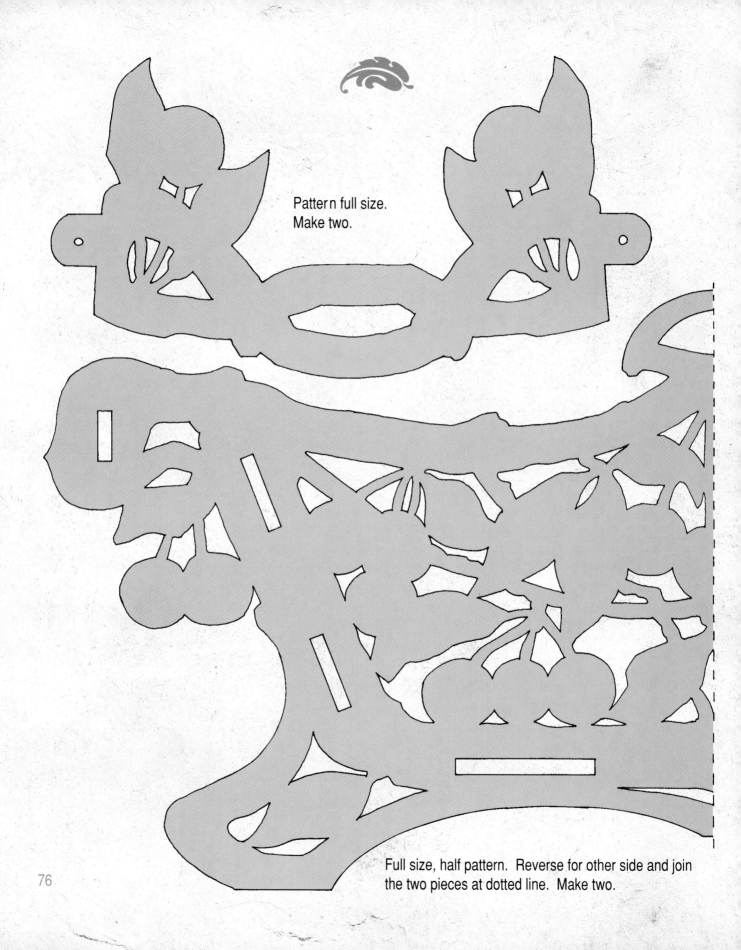

Pattern full size.
Make two.

Full size, half pattern. Reverse for other side and join
the two pieces at dotted line. Make two.

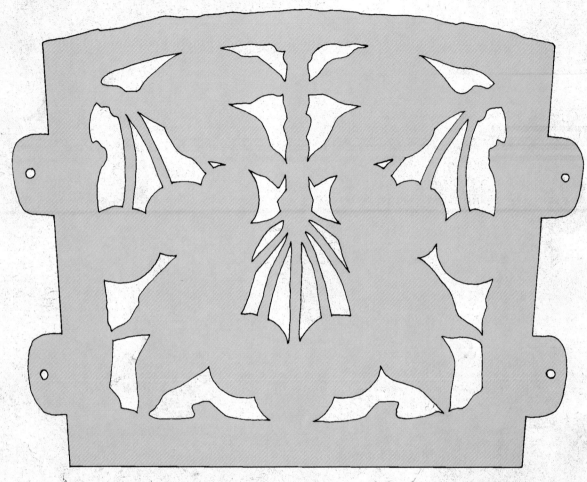

Pattern full size. Make two.

Enlarge bottom panel 200%.
Make one.

I saw the angel
in the marble
and I just chiseled
til I set him free

—Michelangelo

Candle Holders
Gösta Dahlqvist

Top view

Side view

Patterns full size.

Deer Box
Nancy Holewinski

Two small hinges or a piano hinge are recommended for attaching the lid.

Optional methods for making corner joints.

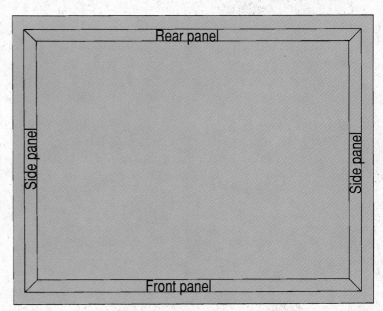

Bottom panel, make one.

Side panels, make two.

Lip parts for lid, make two each

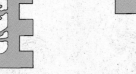

Front leg, make two.

Front panel. Make a second panel the same size without interior cutouts for the rear.

Side leg, make two.

Enlarge patterns 200%.

Pattern full size. Lid, make one.

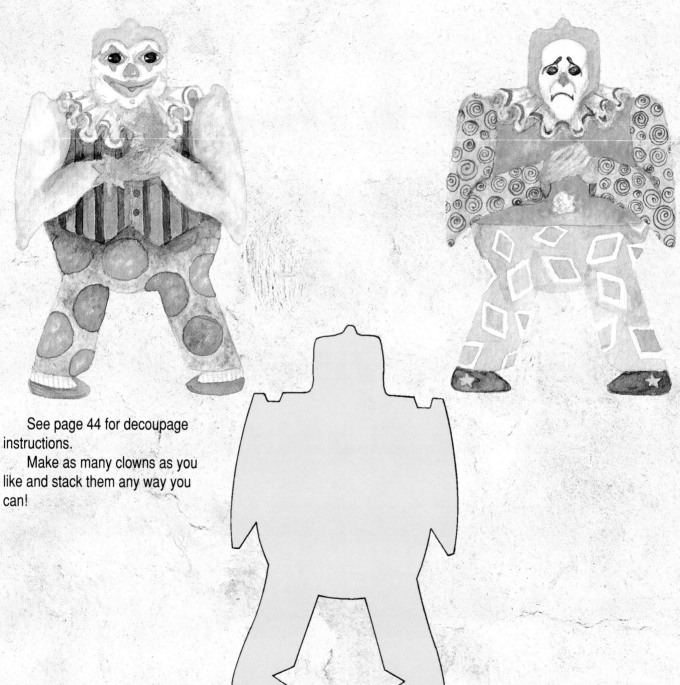

See page 44 for decoupage instructions.

Make as many clowns as you like and stack them any way you can!

Patterns full size.

Butterfly Bookends
Julie Kiehnau

Designed by Patricia Spielman   Pattern full size.

The ¼" thick fretted piece is rabbeted into the surface of one of two ⅝" thick boards before they are glued together. Note the rabbet and round-over router bits. Attach a heavy piece of metal with flat head wood screws to the bottom of the piece.

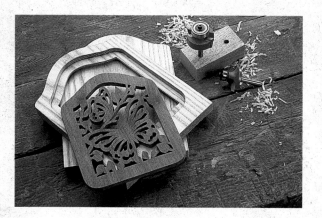

Countersink the metal for no. 7 screws. Apply self-adhesive cork to the bottom of the metal. Metal and cork can be obtained from Meisel Hardware specialties, Mound, Minnesota.

Dolphin Bookends
Julie Kiehnau

Cut from 1" thick hardwood.

Enlarge pattern 200%.

Paisley Bookends
Julie Kiehnau

Done in 1" thick cherry.

Designed by Patricia Spielman   Pattern full size.   89

Kokopelli
Dan Kihl

The base is cut from ½" plywood (patterns found on pages 91 and 92). The kokopellis are cut from ⅛" baltic birch plywood.

Laminate a thin sheet of plywood with copper. Cut the kokopellis, coyote and prickly pear. Cut the inlays in the kokopellis, then laquer. Acid-treat the other pieces and then glue the inlays back in place. Cut out the base and paint black. Lacquer. Glue scene together using numbers and letters as a guide.

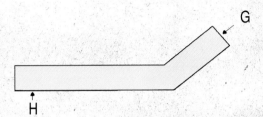

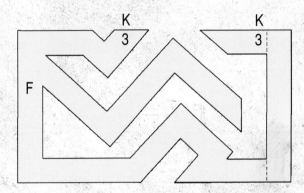

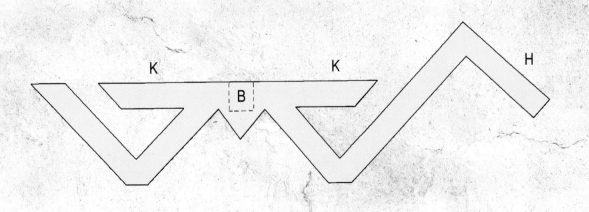

Enlarge patterns 200%.

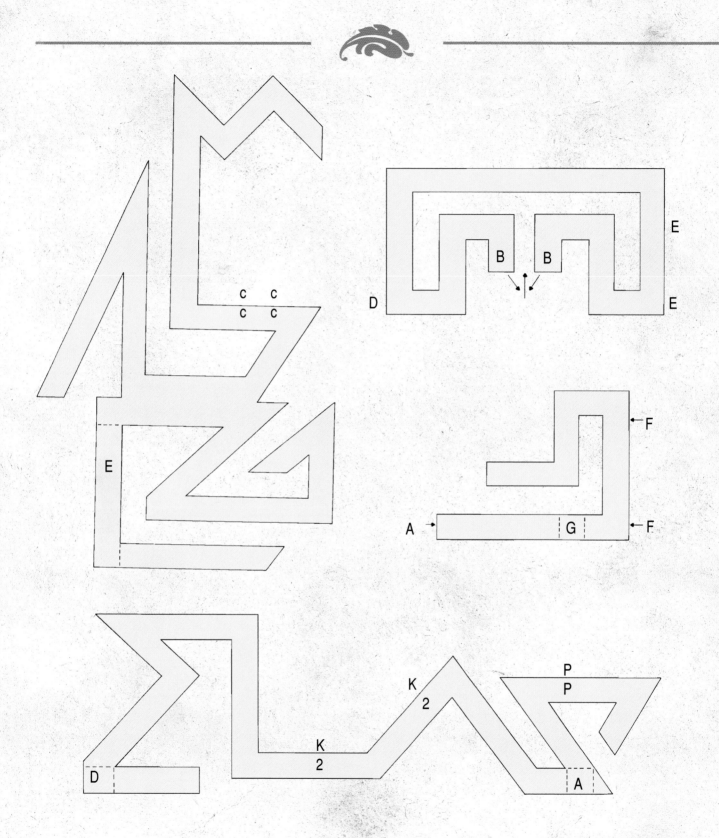

Enlarge patterns 200%.

Mount to base below lines.

Enlarge patterns 200%.

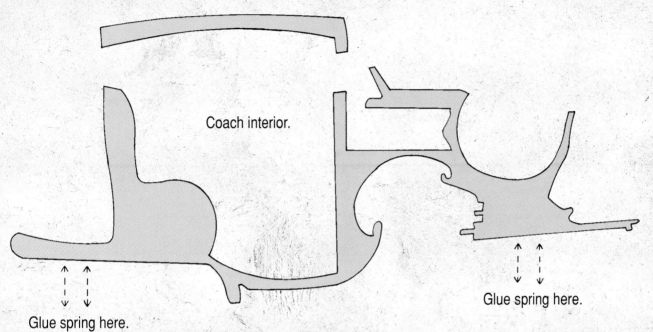

Coach interior.

Glue spring here.

Glue spring here.

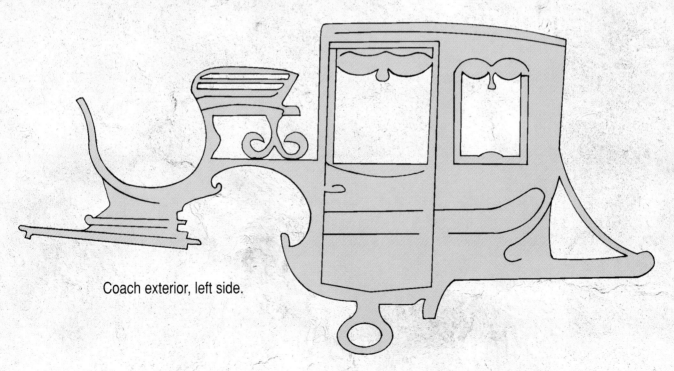

Coach exterior, left side.

Patterns full size.

1/8" dowel rod axles, make two.

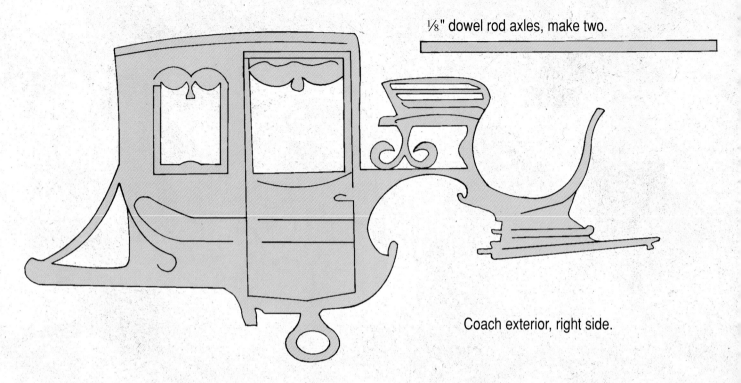

Coach exterior, right side.

Wheels, make four.

Chassis spring, drill 1/8" hole.

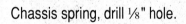

Axle keeper, drill 1/8" hole.

Patterns full size.

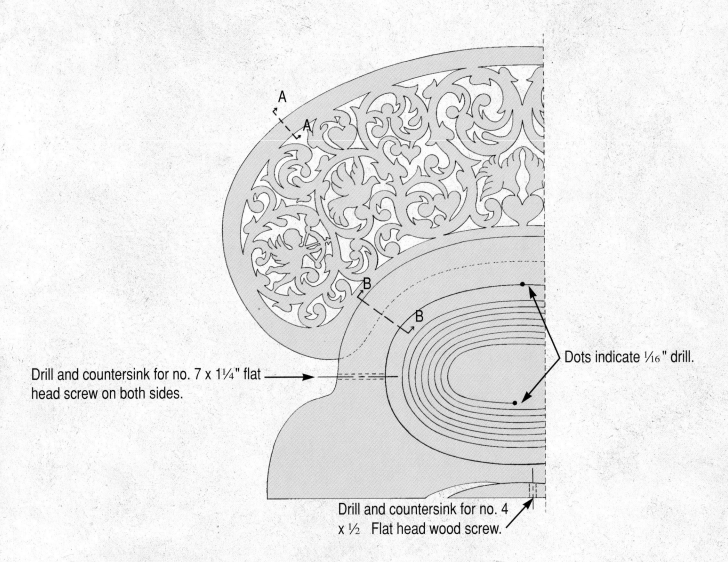

A

A

B

B

Dots indicate ¹⁄₁₆" drill.

Drill and countersink for no. 7 x 1¼" flat head screw on both sides.

Drill and countersink for no. 4 x ½ Flat head wood screw.

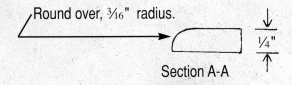

Round over, ³⁄₁₆" radius.

¼"

Section A-A

Enlarge pattern 200%.

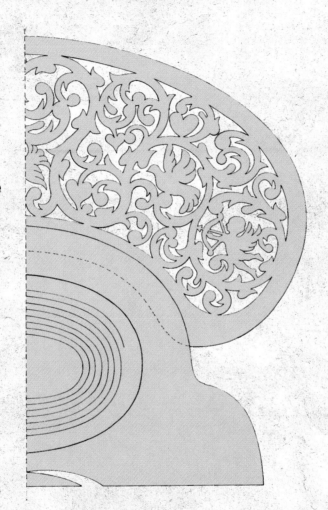

Dashed line indicates where
the two pattern pieces join.

Round over ¼" radius, typical.

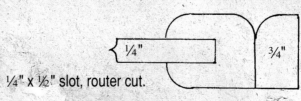

¼"

¾"

¼" x ½" slot, router cut.

Section B-B

Noah's Ark
John and Sheila Polhemus

Enlarge pattern 200%.
Join at solid line.

Sides for top, make two. Enlarge pattern 200%.

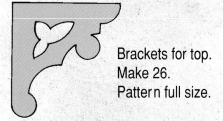

Brackets for top.
Make 26.
Pattern full size.

This pattern is designed for ⅜"-thick material to make the box. Use thinner, contrasting material for overlays for the top (see page 106).

Pattern for top showing correct position of various parts. Connects at solid line to pattern on page 105. Enlarge pattern 200%. Use this pattern, excluding flower designs, for bottom.

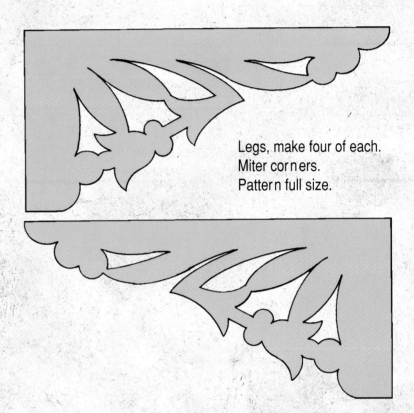

Legs, make four of each.
Miter corners.
Pattern full size.

Ornaments for bottom, make two.
Pattern full size.

Pattern for top. Attach to pattern on page 104 at solid line.
Enlarge pattern 200%.

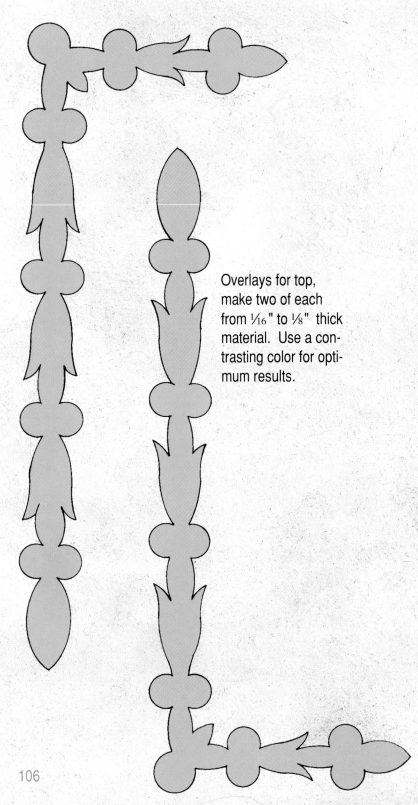

Side panels,
make two.
Enlarge
pattern 200%.

Overlays for top,
make two of each
from $\frac{1}{16}$" to $\frac{1}{8}$" thick
material. Use a con-
trasting color for opti-
mum results.

Standing Frame
Carla Radsek

Center, make one.

Side, make two (one reversed.)

Enlarge pattern 200%.

MATCHES

All other patterns full size.

Miniature Clocks
Kirk Ratajesak

25°

Pattern is full size for the mini
clock. To make the larger clock,
enlarge pattern 200%.

Candelabra
James Reidle

Use ¼" material. Be aware that the thickness of plywood or solid wood may vary slightly (most often undersize) and may require slight pattern adjustments to the slotted area and halved joints to prevent pieces from fitting together too loosely.

Extra care should be taken to prevent breakage. Double check the thickness of the material you are using by placing it on edge in the slotted area of the pattern and tracing the width to ensure a perfect fit. We recommend sawing the long-halves slot last as it leaves the upper section temporarily weakened until assembly.

Use glue only for joining parts wherever possible, but discreet use of nail and screw (with glue) may also be desired.

Do not use excess glue that may squeeze out. Any glue remaining on visible surfaces will seal the wood so that finishes will not penetrate.

Candle cups are available and should be attached with small screws.

Top for base. Join base halves and secure in position on tabs.

Bottom for upper section. Join upper-section halves and secure in position on tabs.

Ornament for middle candle.

Ornament for other candles. Make four.

Candle stand. Make four.

Enlarge patterns 200%.

Base halves.

Enlarge patterns 200%.

Upper section, half.

Enlarge pattern 200%.

Upper section, half.

Enlarge patterns 200%.

Lidded Work Basket
Jim Reidle

Suggested material: 5/16"-thick solid wood for optimum results. If availability is limited, substitutions can be made, but will require pattern adjustments.

Special care should be taken to attain a perfect fit for tabs and slots. Since the thickness of wood may vary slightly (most often undersize), we recommend tracing the thickness of the material you will use directly onto the pattern for the slots. This will provide more accurate lines for precise sawing. Sand and pre-fit various parts (where practical) before making interior cutouts. This could avoid ruining a piece by an error in fitting the tab and slot after sawing all the cutouts.

Fitting the lid requires extra attention. Rounding over the edges nearest the center divider will provide necessary clearance for opening and closing. Using 1/8"-diameter dowels provides hinging of the lids. You may need an extra pair of hands to hold the side panels and lids in position while drilling the holes for the dowels.

End panels are beveled at top and bottom to fit. Instead of making the cuts by a saw, a beltsander, discsander, or small hand plane can also be used.

Side panels, make two. Enlarge pattern 200%.

Bottom panel. Enlarge pattern 200%.

Center divider with handle.
Enlarge pattern 200%.

End panels, make two.
Bevel top and bottom.
Pattern full size.

Lids, make two. Round over edges to provide clearance for opening.
Pattern full size.

Instarsia Santa
Judy Gale Roberts

Recommended wood: western red cedar, ¾" thick. Join with pattern on page 122 at solid line.

You can simplify this pattern by drawing the robe and white trim parts on one piece of white wood (making the grain direction all of the same way), then cutting it into the separate sections. The areas marked with "M" can be stained red. Roberts mixes her own stain by using artist oil paint with an oil-based clear sealer (Bartley wiping gel is also recommended).

LEGEND
←——→	Grain direction
D	Dark shade of wood
MD	Medium-dark shade of wood
M	Medium shade of wood
LT	Light shade of wood
W	White pine or any white wood

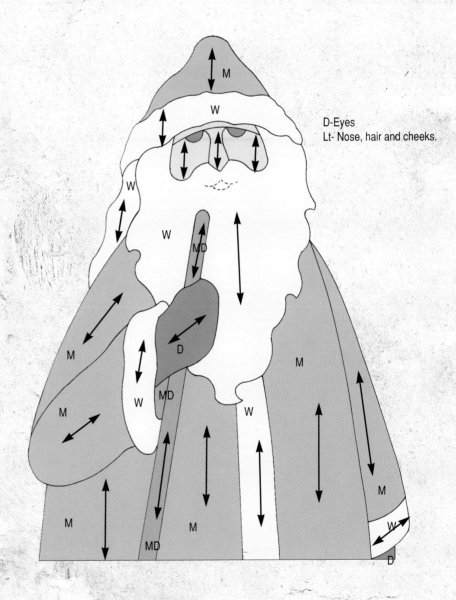

D-Eyes
Lt- Nose, hair and cheeks.

Enlarge pattern 200%.
© 1991 Judy Gale Roberts

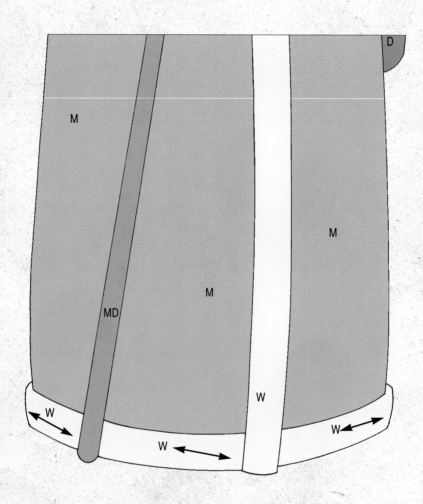

Enlarge pattern 200%.
© 1991 Judy Gale Roberts

Napkin and Candle Holders
Kim and Rob Russell

Side piece, cut two of hardwood, ¼" x 4" x 13".
Sand smooth. Glue blocks onto one side, then the
other. Enlarge pattern 200%.

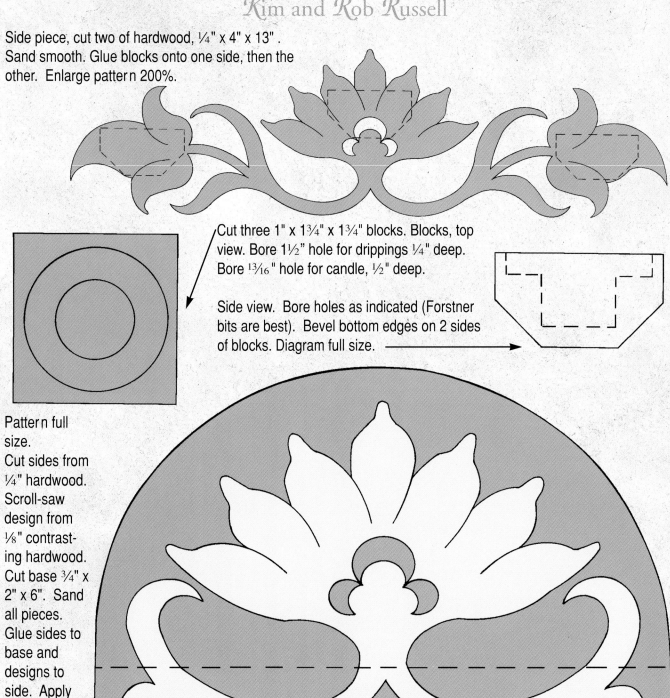

Cut three 1" x 1¾" x 1¾" blocks. Blocks, top
view. Bore 1½" hole for drippings ¼" deep.
Bore $^{13}/_{16}$" hole for candle, ½" deep.

Side view. Bore holes as indicated (Forstner
bits are best). Bevel bottom edges on 2 sides
of blocks. Diagram full size.

Pattern full
size.
Cut sides from
¼" hardwood.
Scroll-saw
design from
⅛" contrast-
ing hardwood.
Cut base ¾" x
2" x 6". Sand
all pieces.
Glue sides to
base and
designs to
side. Apply
finish.

Train Puzzle
Gus Stefureac

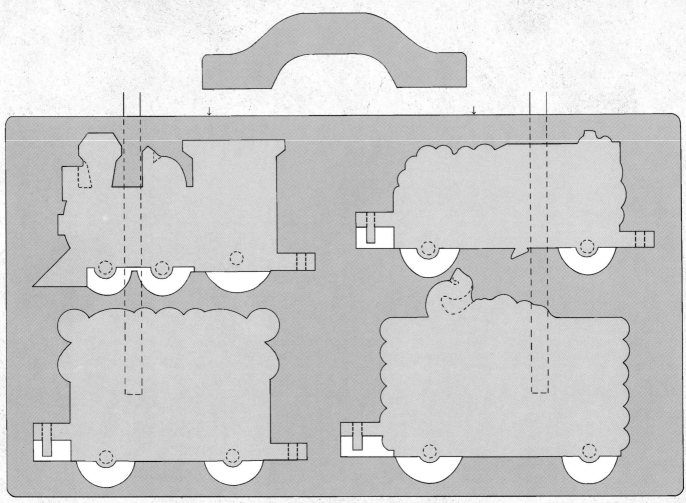

Recommended wood: 1¹⁄₁₆" thick maple.
16 wheels 1" in diameter.
2 wheels 1¼" in diameter.
Toy axle pegs to fit wheels.
2 dowels ³⁄₈" in diameter.
4 pegs ½" long and ¼" in diameter.

   Pattern shows placement for pegs and dowels. Drill holes to loosely fit dowels and axles, following pattern as a guide. Drill holes at front of cars to tightly fit coupler pegs. Glue pegs in place. Attach carryinghandle as shown with screws.

   Follow decoupage instructions on page 44 to decorate. Paint carrier as desired, to match artwork.

   Lastly, mount all wheels. Carefully glue to axles.

Enlarge pattern 200%.

Black Forest Clock
Carl Weckhorst

Positions of parts that attach to the back panel are indicated.

2. ¼" solid, cut two

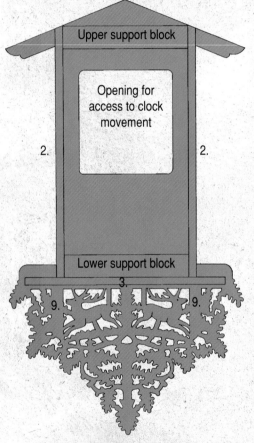

Upper support block

Opening for access to clock movement

2.   2.

Lower support block

3.

9.   9.

1. Back panel

Lower support block

2.

Opening for pendulum

5.   4.

3. Bottom panel

4. Front panel

Enlarge patterns 200%.

5. Overlay for front
Use ⅛"-thick material.

6. Roof, cut two

7. Overlay on
wood bob
Not on a brass
bob. ⅛"-thick
material.

10. Front railing

8. Gable ornament

11. Overlay on
piece 2, ⅛" thick

12. Make two

9. Support brackets,
make two.

Enlarge patterns 200%.

Gallery

Fish by Donald Frechette. This piece is an example of using a scroll saw to cut plastic.

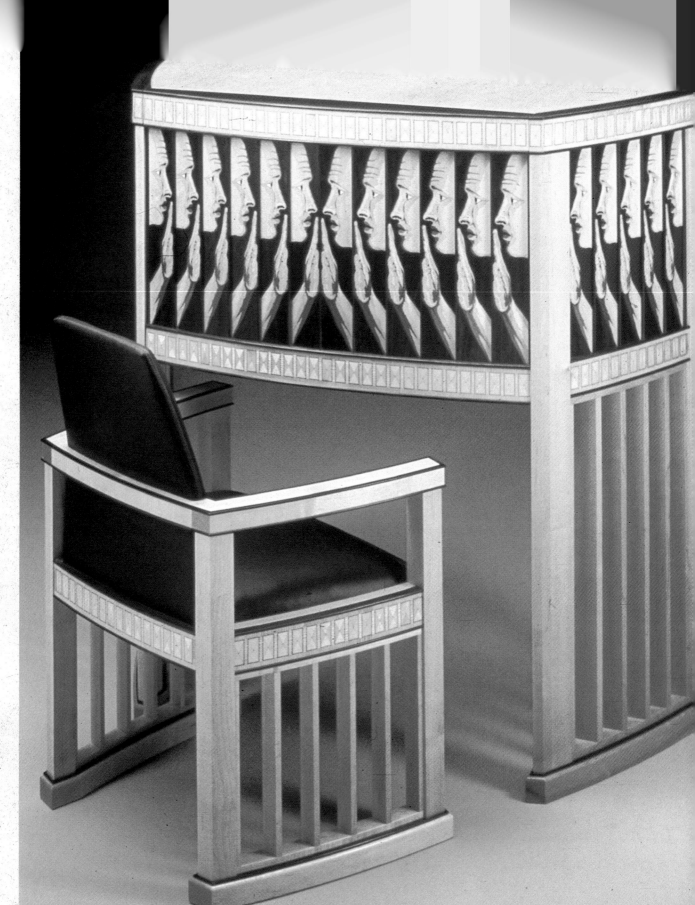

Violin Master cabinet by Silas Kopf.

Pyramid puzzle by Steve Malavolta.

Circular puzzle by Steve Malavolta.

Rectangular interchangeable puzzles by Steve Malavolta.

Samuri by Jeff Nelson.

The Higher Ground by Jeff Nelson.

Clock by Jim Reidle.

Eiffle Tower by Jim Reidle.

Fire Engine Clock by Jim Reidle and Carl Weckhorst.

Defender Clock by Jim Reidle, Sr.

Muh Dear by Judy Gale Roberts.

Hidden Forest by Judy Gale Roberts.

Detail of Seaside Retreat by James Shirley and Sons.

The Church Goers by James Shirley and Sons.

Detail of Todd at the scroll saw working on the Galveston, Texas, Porch. Each piece in the "paintings" are individually sawn.

Each piece of wood in these "paintings" is selected for its unique color. The Shirley's do not paint their wood–they use Mother Nature's palate.

Resident Wizard by Hal Smith.

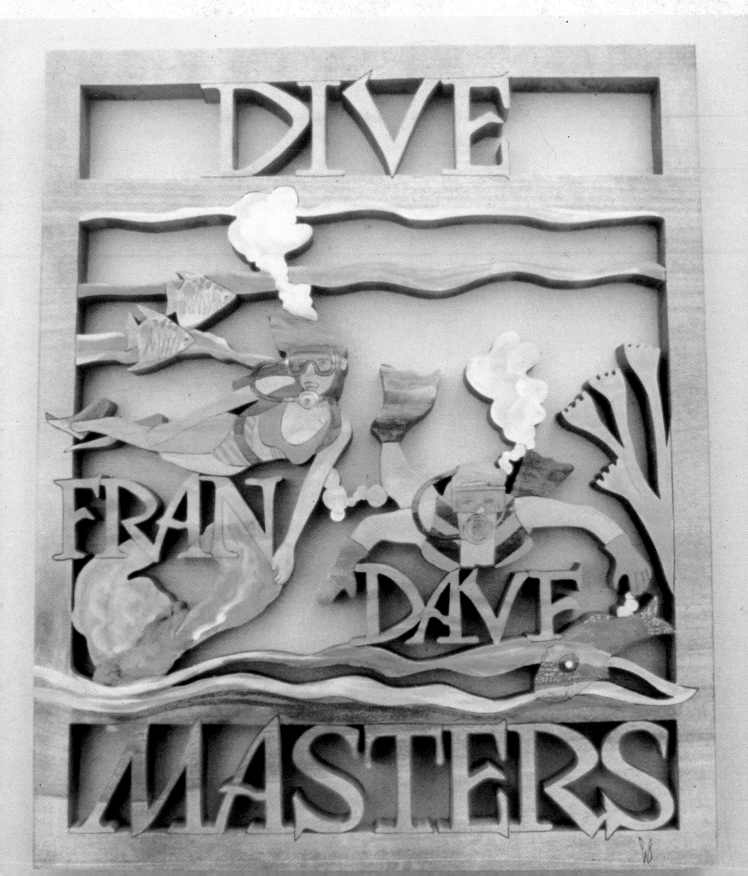

Eye of the Great Spirit by Gerald Wheeler.

Buffalo Storm bowl and Hopi Dancer
by Gerald Wheeler.

Flight of Fancy wall grid by Robin Wirtz.

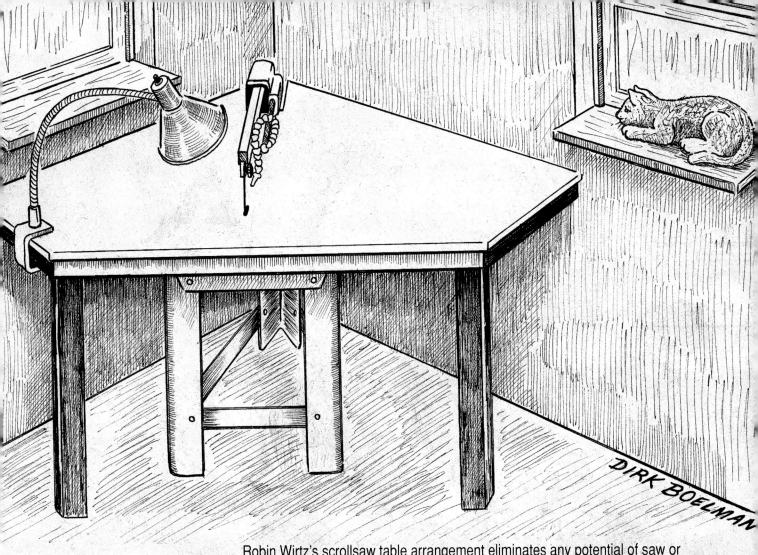

Robin Wirtz's scrollsaw table arrangement eliminates any potential of saw or machine vibration from being transferred to her very delicate workpieces. The machine is bolted to the floor. Her worktable is independent (not touching the machine). It is bolted to the wall. The large plastic laminated work surface provides a working radius that's more than equal to the throat capacity of the saw.

Magnolia
and
Sunface
tabletops
by Marc
Young.

Index

Metric Equivalency Chart

MM-Millimetres CM-Centimetres

INCHES TO MILLIMETRES AND CENTIMETRES

INCHES	MM	CM	INCHES	CM	INCHES	CM
⅛	3	0.3	9	22.9	30	76.2
¼	6	0.6	10	25.4	31	78.7
½	13	1.3	12	30.5	33	83.8
⅝	16	1.6	13	33.0	34	86.4
¾	19	1.9	14	35.6	35	88.9
⅞	22	2.2	15	38.1	36	91.4
1	25	2.5	16	40.6	37	94.0
1¼	32	3.2	17	43.2	38	96.5
1½	38	3.8	18	45.7	39	99.1
1¾	44	4.4	19	48.3	40	101.6
2	51	5.1	20	50.8	41	104.1
2½	64	6.4	21	53.3	42	106.7
3	76	7.6	22	55.9	43	109.2
3½	89	8.9	23	58.4	44	111.8
4	102	10.2	24	61.0	45	114.3
4½	114	11.4	25	63.5	46	116.8
5	127	12.7	26	66.0	47	119.4
6	152	15.2	27	68.6	48	121.9
7	178	17.8	28	71.1	49	124.5
8	203	20.3	29	73.7	50	127.0